David, we're PREGNANT!

101 cartoons for
Expecting Parents
by Lynn Johnston

Stoddart

ISBN 0-7737-5055-X

First published in 1985 by
Stoddart Publishing Co. Limited
34 Lesmill Road
Toronto, Canada
M38 2T6

First published in the United States by
Simon & Schuster Inc.
1230 Avenue of the Americas
New York, N.Y. 10020
U.S.A.

10   9   8   7   6   5   4   3

Printed and bound in the United States

I'm pretty sure that I am....
but what if I'm not.... what if
it's negative... or nerves... or
imagination. Actually, I'm
positive I am. I'll phone
for a checkup. But what
if they tell me I'm not....
better wait another week
to make sure..... No. Why
wait if I'm POSITIVE!....
Then again... what if I'm not....
On the other hand...
maybe.........

LYNN

I don't understand it, Dad... Jan just found out she's pregnant—but I'm the one with the knots in my stomach!
Lynn

Well, congratulations, Elly!..... You know, Lewis & I would have had children...but, we just don't have the patience.
LYNN

35

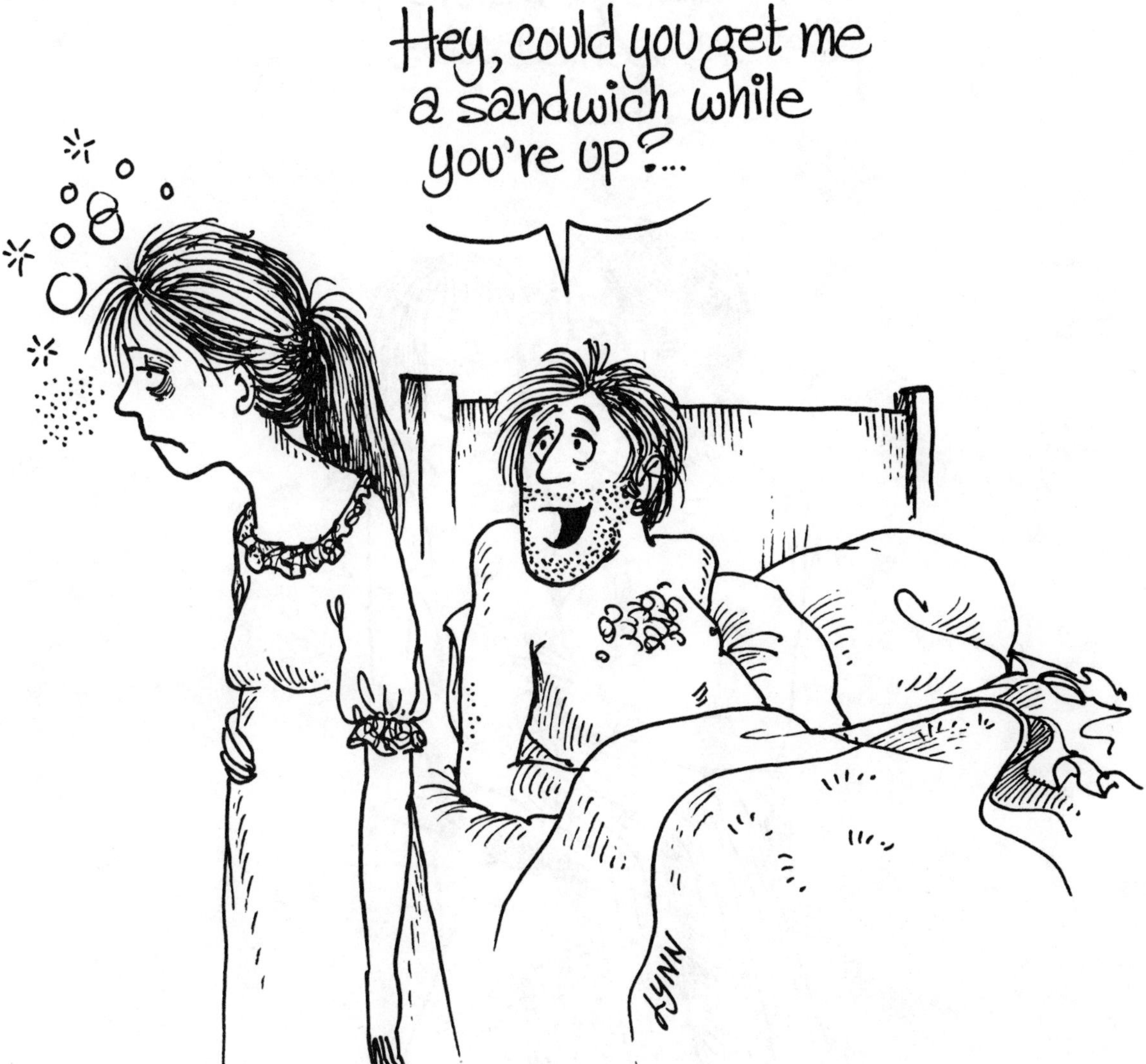
Hey, could you get me a sandwich while you're up?...
LYNN

48

49

50

51

53

Mom, Ken's agreed to go to prenatal classes with Barbie....

Lynn

59

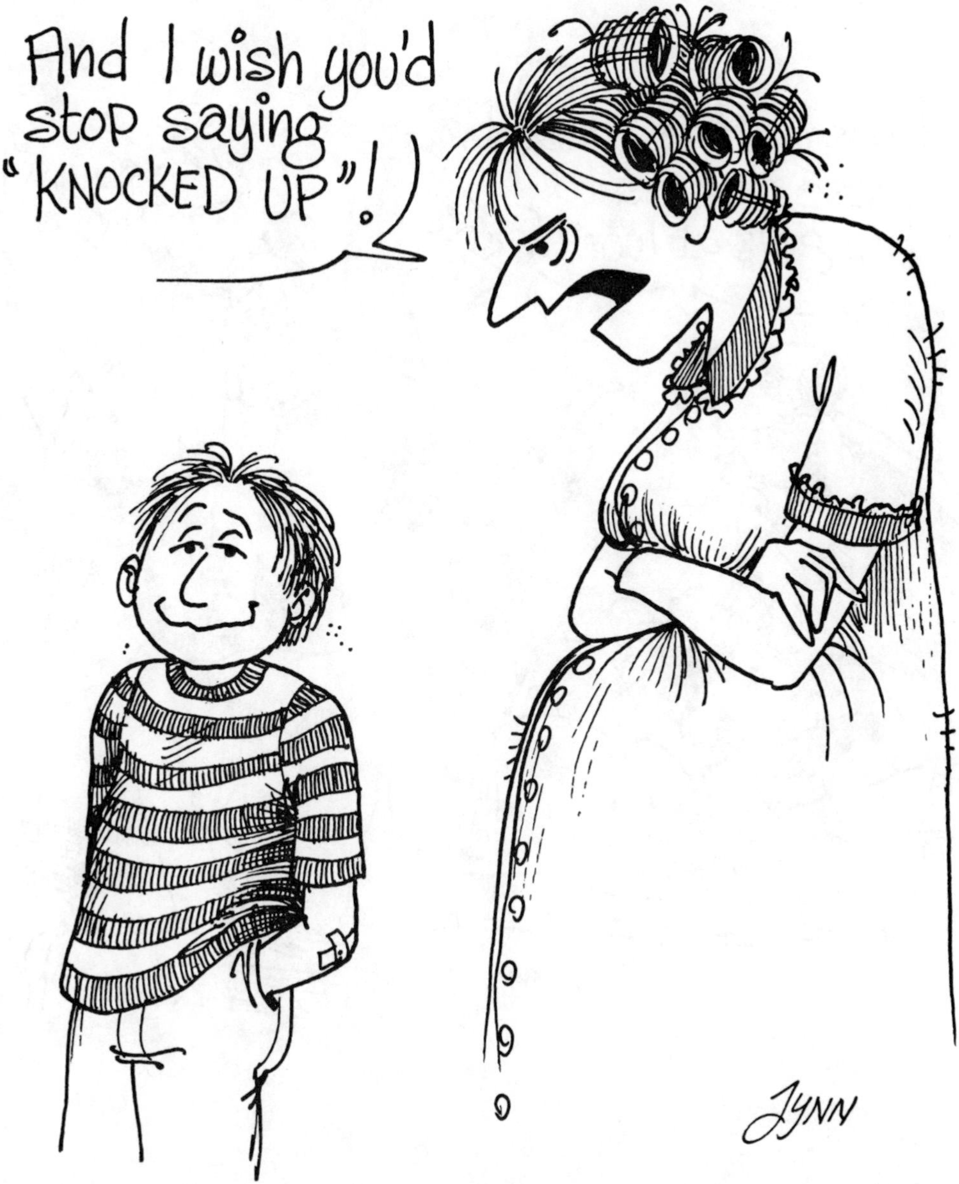
And I wish you'd stop saying "KNOCKED UP"!
LYNN

64

While you're waddling around town- could you pick me up a copy of the evening edition?
LYNN

69

71

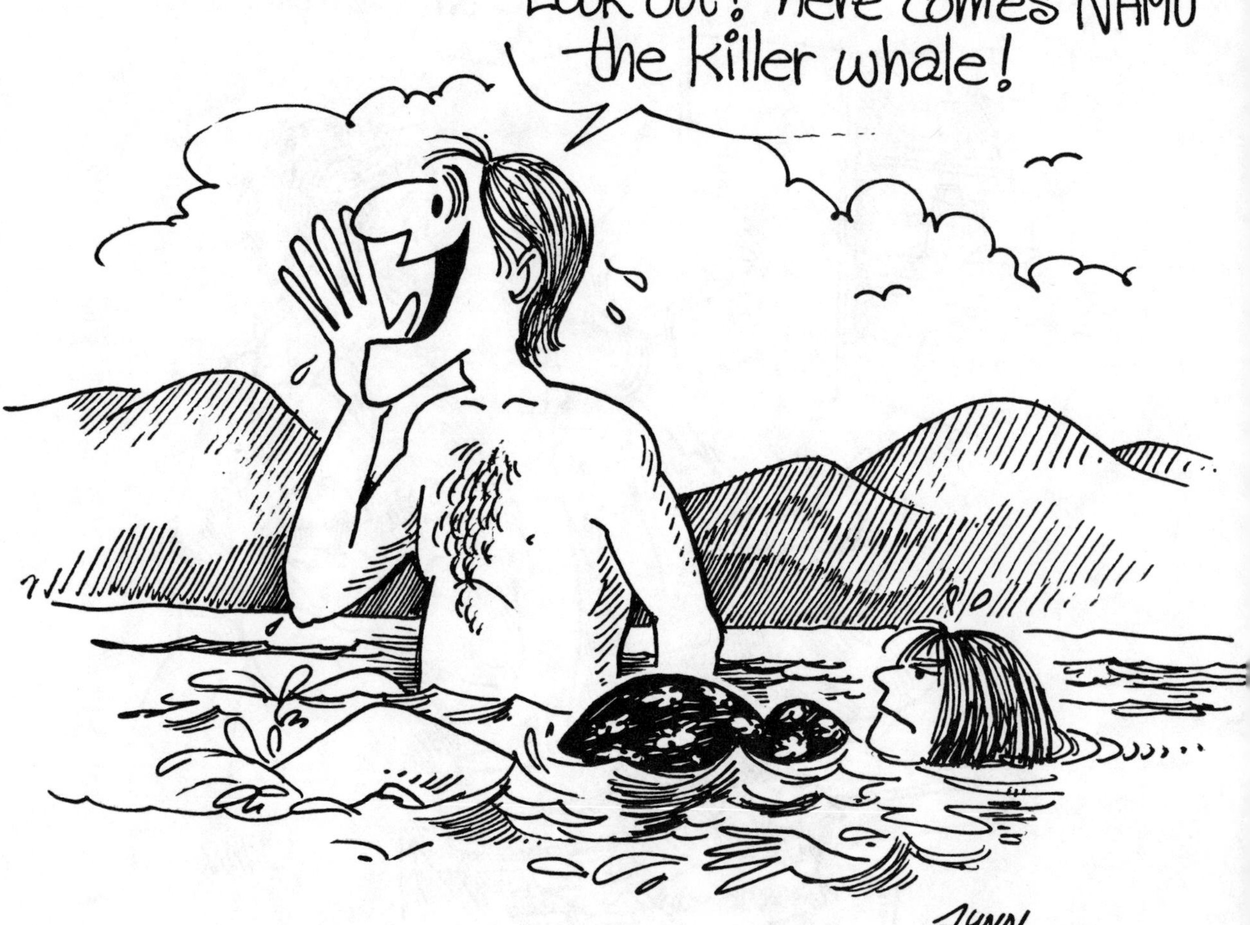
Look out! here comes NAMU the killer whale!
LYNN

73

No matter how I lie, I'm uncomfortable.... I think I'm going to have to learn how to sleep standing up.
ZZZZ
LYNN

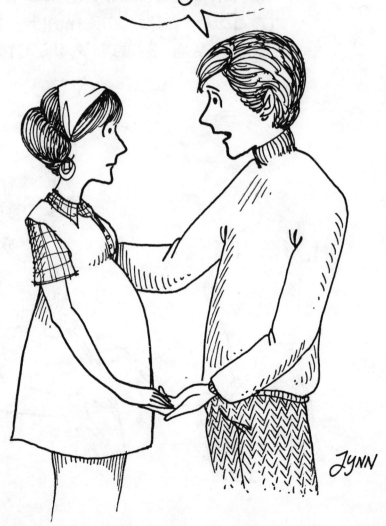

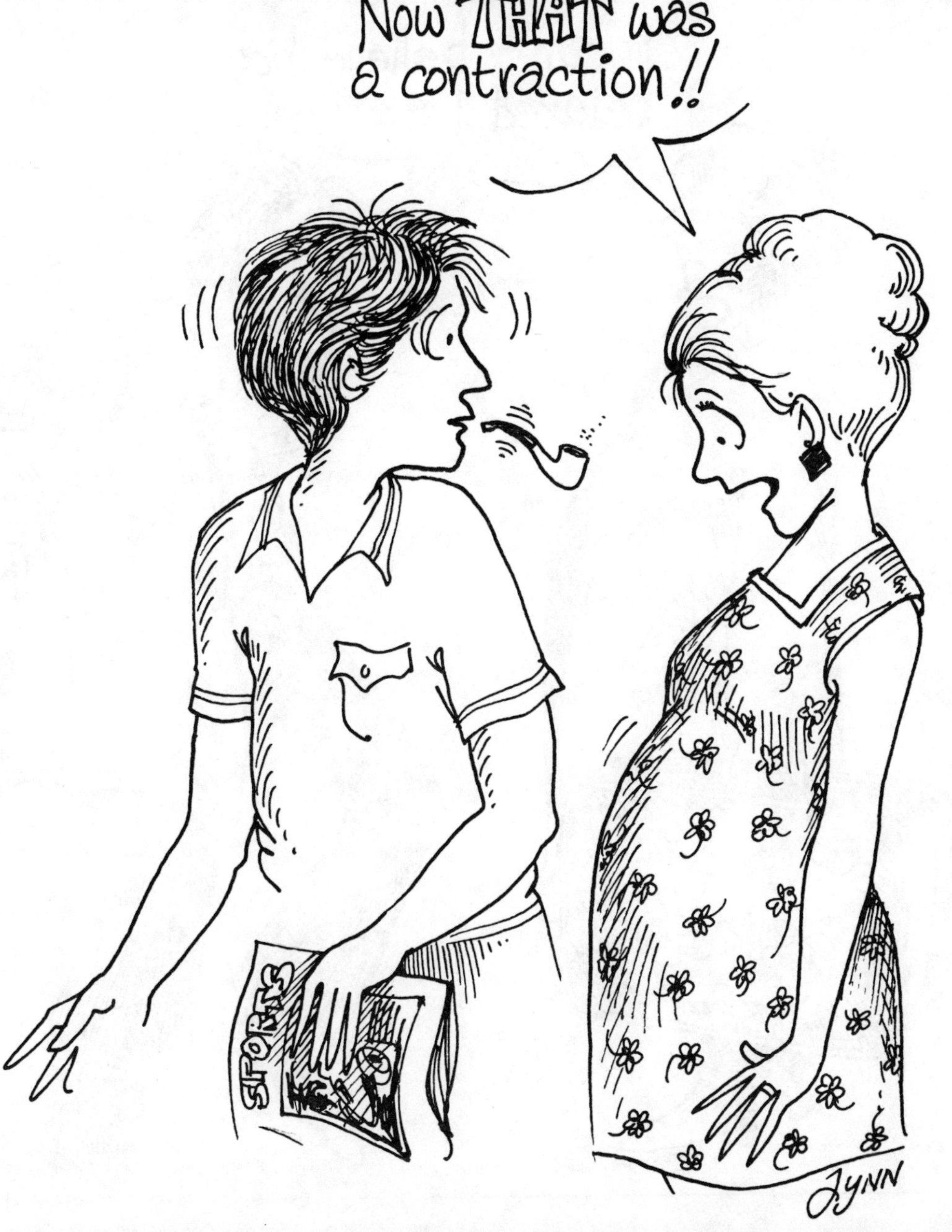
Now THAT was a contraction!!
SPORTS
LYNN

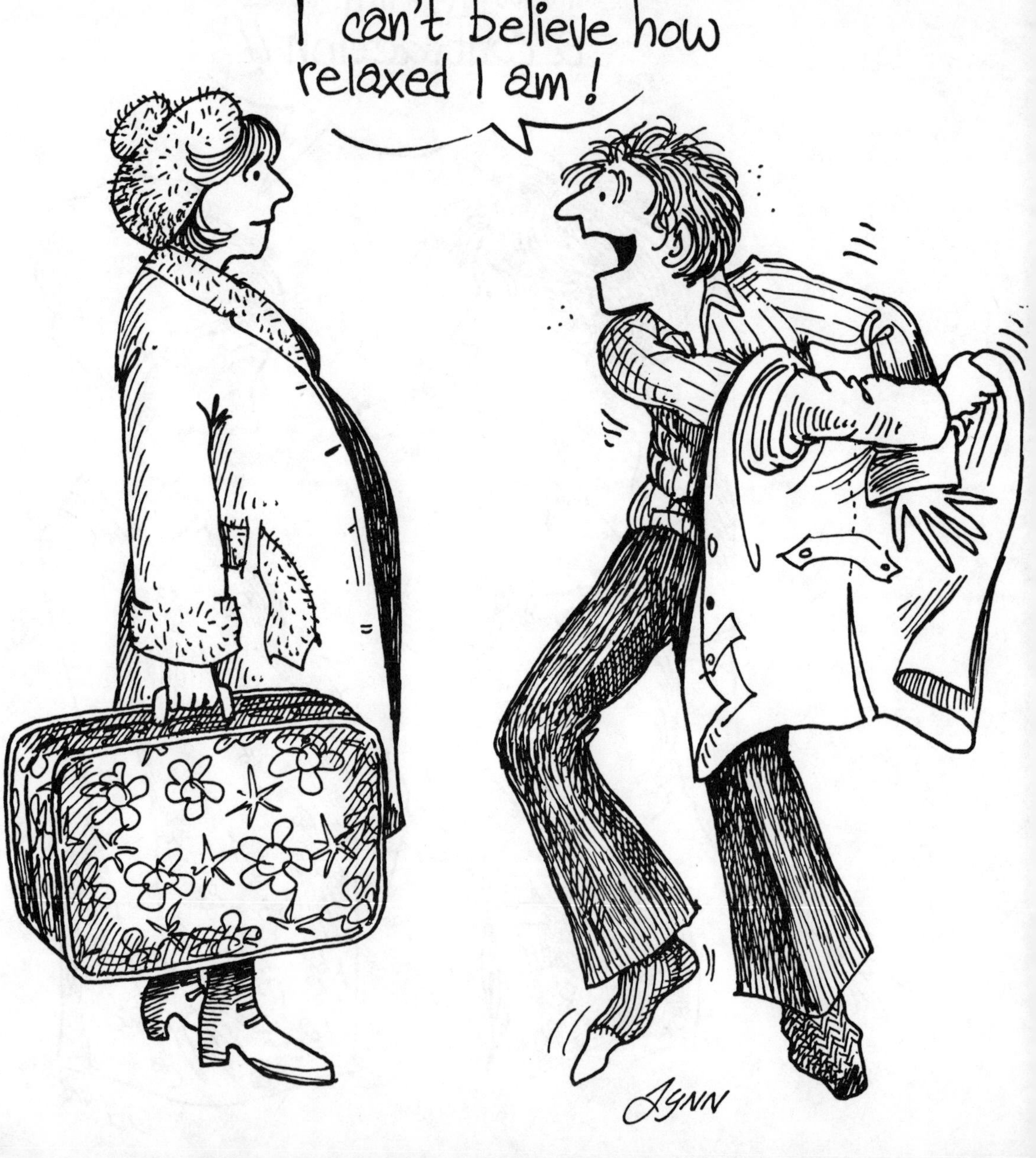
I can't believe how relaxed I am!
LYNN

82

84

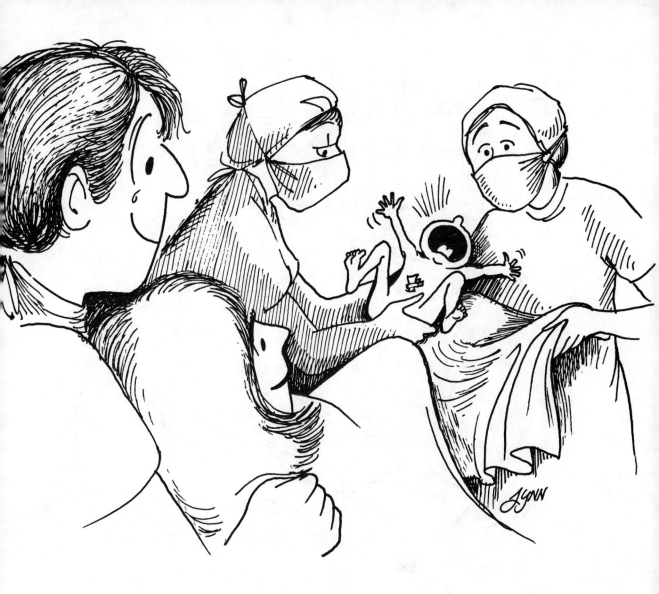

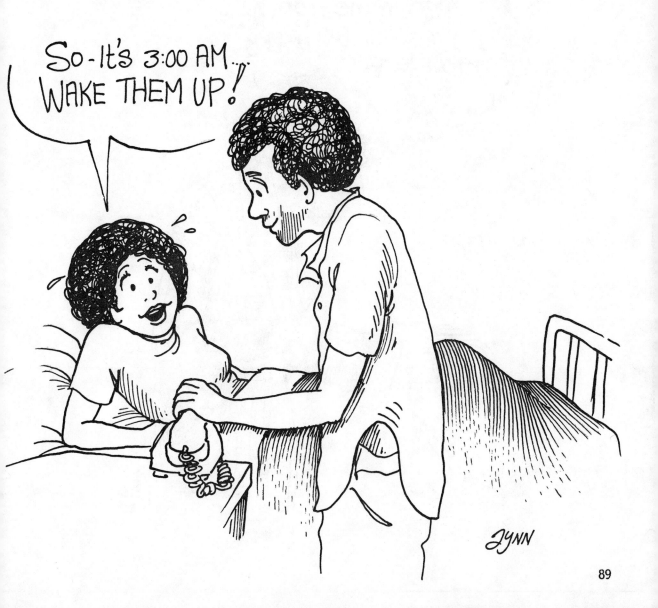

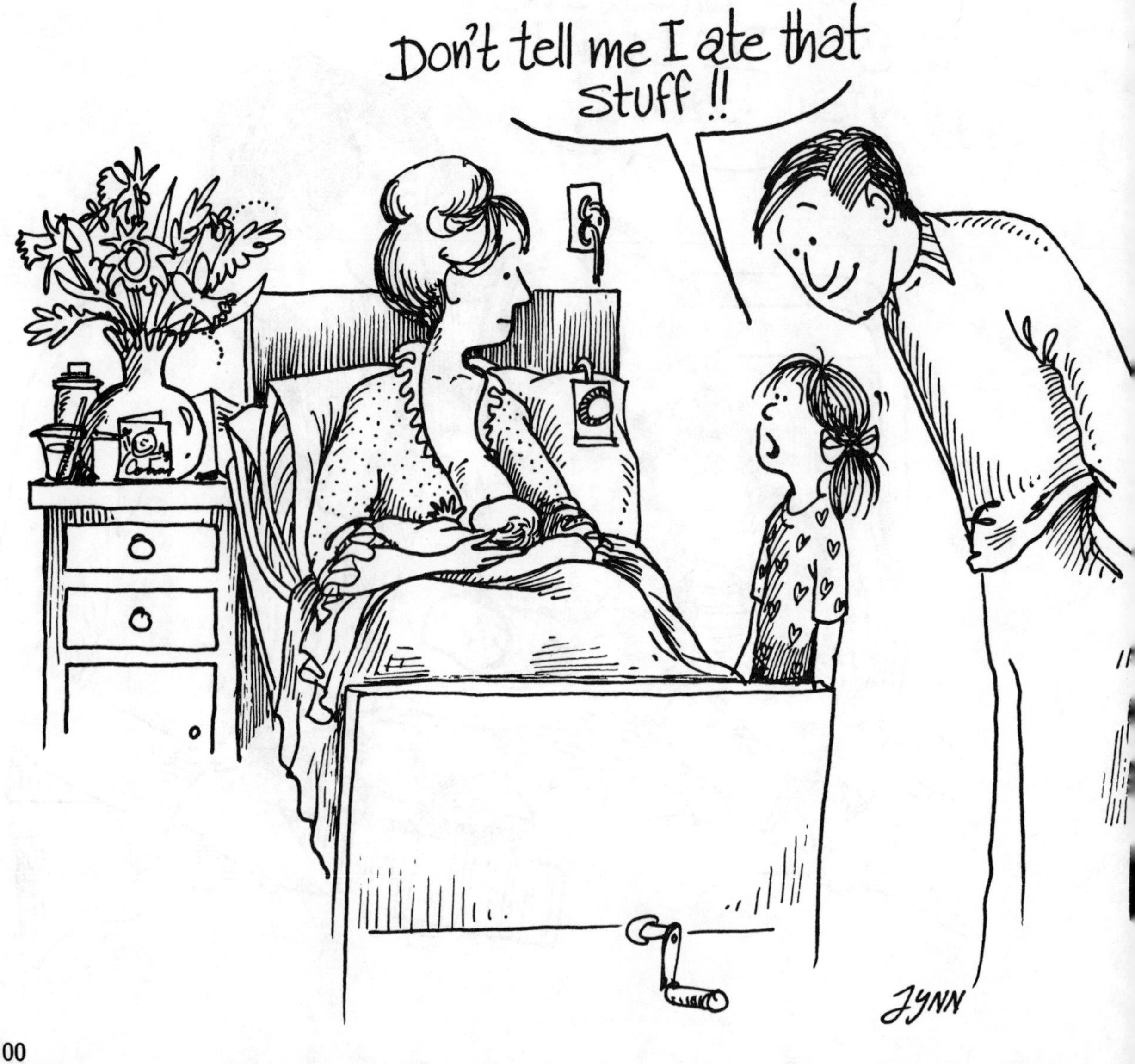
Don't tell me I ate that STUFF !!
JYNN

Meet Lynn Johnston

Lynn Johnston is the best-selling female cartoonist in North America with good reason. She draws much of her material from close observation of her family—Aaron, Katie, and husband Roderick, a "flying dentist" whose practice is based in Lynn Lake (no relation), 800 miles north of Winnipeg, Manitoba. Her deft, humorous depictions of life with kids have provided her with material for three books, published by Meadowbrook, and now she has a family comic strip, "For Better or For Worse" running in newspapers throughout North America.

& Her Books:

DAVID WE'RE PREGNANT!!

101 laughing out loud cartoons that accentuate the humorous side of conceiving, expecting and giving birth. A great baby shower gift, it's the perfect way to bolster the spirits of any expectant couple.

0-7737-5055-X

HI MOM! HI DAD!

A side splitting sequel to DAVID WE'RE PREGNANT! 101 cartoons on the first year of childrearing . . . . . . all those late night wakings, early morning wakings, and other traumatic "emergencies" too numerous to list.

0-7737-5054-1

DO THEY EVER GROW UP?

This third in her series of cartoon books is a hilarious survival guide for parents of the tantrum and pacifier set, as well as a side splitting memory book for parents who have lived through it.

0-7737-1046-9